CAT GOT MY BRAIN
ONE HUNDRED MAD POEMS

D.L. FORBES

FOURBEESBOOKS

Poetry series

London, Edinburgh & San Francisco

ISBN: 978-1-66782-088-0

eBook ISBN: 978-1-66782-089-7

1. Poems of madness - Poetry 2. Mental instability 3. poetry retail

FOURBEESBOOKS

Poetry series

London, Edinburgh & San Francisco

BOOKS BY D. L. FORBES

SAXONFORD
VOLUME ONE
WINTER INTO SUMMER
Fiction

SAXONFORD
VOLUME TWO
SUMMER INTO WINTER
Fiction

CHILDREN OF SYCORAX
Fiction/Biography

LIFE THREATENING POETRY ACROSS AMERICA
ONE HUNDRED ONE DOLLAR POEMS
The One Hundred Poetry Series – Number One

UMLUNGU
THE WHITE SCUM THAT FLOATS IN THE SURF
ONE HUNDRED EVERYDAY POEMS
The One Hundred Poetry Series – Number Two

YID UN GOY YINGL
Fiction/Biography/

GENTILE AND JEW BOYS
ONE HUNDRED POEMS FOR SHEM
The One Hundred Poetry Series – Number Three

ROUGH FLUFF
ONE HUNDRED LOVE POEMS
The One Hundred Poetry Series – Number Four

CHARMED, I'M SURE
ONE HUNDRED SEXUAL POEMS
The One Hundred Poetry Series – Number Five

WITTGENSTEIN'S SON
&
U. G. KRISHNAMURTI
DUCKS OR RABBITS
Autobiography/Biography

CAT GOT MY BRAIN
ONE HUNDRED MAD POEMS
The One Hundred Poetry Series – Number Six

THREE PLAYS
I. BABY
II. RUNS IN THE FAMILY
III. LAND'S END

My father

L.J.J.W

In Memoriam

26th April 1889 – 28th April 1951

INTRODUCTION

From the ultra-demented to the almost imperceptibly disturbed, we all suffer; we are all victims of birth, all victims of fearful not far off insanity. Many people however, throughout their entire lives manage to hide their insanity well enough; but there is no getting away from it. With our mind working in high or low degrees of mental, this is who we are, this is how we exist, and living in the unnatural way we do, is it any wonder we are all going or already mad?

An awkward aspect of acknowledged mental illness, is remembering you have a mental illness, and when in the throes, knowing that there are potentially positive 'things' you really need to do about it; but you are unable to do the 'things' you know you need to do, to do something about it. Either because you are too mental right now, or do not care enough about yourself or anything else, or you have forgotten what the mysterious 'things' are – if you ever really knew or had any grasp on these 'things' in the first place.

Well, what can you do when the mental is upon you: run on the spot, open your cognitive therapy instruction manual for the thousandth time, take your a.m. and p.m. meds together, squeeze the pussy for a bit of love, or take your mental-dog out for yet one more last leak? All good, but useless stuff when you come finally to face your mind with yourself.

I do not face my mind's mental self too much these days; for if I did, I would be deader and pressed flatter than one of those long dead creatures on a road, so I busy myself by therapy painting and therapy writing instead, when I remember.

Over the decades I have jotted out poem-like excrescences into hundreds of notebooks and other unlikely surfaces – the back of a cereal box or in my Granny's passport. Thousands of these poems have seeped from my every orifice, and one day, to prevent my mind exploding or lingering on any pressing need for incarceration and electrodes, I decided to sit on the floor for any number of months and put my poems in some order – and soon discovered that they fit into six main categories:

1. Dollar Poems – *Life Threatening Poetry Across America.*
2. Everyday Poems – *Umlungu – The White Scum That Floats in the Surf.*
3. Shem Poems – *Gentile and Jew Boys.*
4. Love Poems – *Charmed, I'm Sure.*
5. Sex Poems – *Rough Fluff.*
6. Mad Poems – *Cat Got My Brain.*

I then picked just one hundred poems from each category, with overlaps, almost but not quite at random, for my life is no longer long enough nor my brain quite up to the task of considering the ins and outs and merits or otherwise of a few thousand poems – six hundred poems then, in six poetry books.

All this I now feel, has been a slightly better alternative and more productive than murdering oneself, or running amuck and riding naked down busy Market Street in a shopping cart while waving one's trusty meat cleaver in the air, or alternately, taking up a career in politics.

D. L. Forbes – November 2021

CAT GOT MY BRAIN

CONTENTS

1.

IXX. My Policeman Friend – Halftime Sociopath

My policeman friend paused from masticating popcorn to look at me

"Do you think you might be a sociopath?" he asked.

"No," I replied, "but thank you for asking."

"I think you might be a sociopath."

"Oh, well, okay. You're the policeman and obviously directly conversant with a sociopathic temperament."

"I am."

Good . . . and?"

"Nothing . . . only I was just wondering if you might need locking up."

"Why?" I said, lowering my book and looking at him. "Because I would rather sit here and read a book while you watch your game on the telly."

"It's an important game."

"Yes, I know it is, and your team is losing and you're fractious and need to take your loutish frustration out on some innocent bystander."

"Well, I think it's just kinda rude, you reading while there's an important game going on right in front of you. We've got to win this game to get through to the semi-finals."

"I told you before the game started, I'd go and read out on the patio."

"I don't want you to read on the patio, I want you here with me on the couch . . . the chips and dip and stuff are in here anyway."

"So what do you want me to do? Do you want me to watch the game with you?"

"Yes, I do. You sitting there reading might just jinx the whole game for us."

"Are you serious?"

"Well, who knows . . . you don't know that it won't. You can't say for sure one way or the other it won't."

"All right," I said putting the book aside. "I'll watch the game with you, and Anita Brookner will just have to wait; she can chew gum and charmingly squirt spit with the guys in their sidelines bunker thingy."

"It's called a *dugout* . . . and *no* women allowed in the dugout."

The game got underway again.

"*Go! Go!*" my policeman friend shouted at the screen.

"That one swinging his long club," I commented, "has a really great shaped arse."

My policeman friend looked silent sideways daggers at me.

"Well, he does," I protested, "*Tres* callipygous."

"*Come on! Come on!*" my policeman friend shouted at the screen.

"Wow!" I exclaimed enthusiastically. "Look at the muscular thighs on that stud, I wouldn't mind going for a bit of a touchdown with that one . . . a scrumptious scrum there alright."

"*Please*," my policeman friend looked at me aghast, "this is baseball . . . there are *no* touchdowns."

"Well, maybe they should include a few, just to make it a bit more interesting, a bit more homo inclusive, and homoerotic."

"Just shut-up and read your book, okay?"

"Oh, okay."

"And please, go do it outside . . . *and*," he shouted after me, "you can take that cap off too! I'm not buying the team's baseball cap for no English jinxes!"

2.

To Doctor's H' and S'

Doctor H'
As slick and as cool
As a twelve-inch cucumber.

I allow him to plug me in
Let him zap me away –
A man to never blow my fuse.

He takes away my sights
Takes away my noises –
Leaving me staring and amazed – I thank him.

Doctor S'
As cool and as slick
As a fifteen-inch cucumber.

With his life-saving surgical skills
Snips and tucks, forceps and drills
His syringe technique pack seismic thrills.

For serving the needy
Refreshing the seedy
Transforming the He's into She's – I thank him.

3.

Edison's Medicine – I

The moment I loathe after ECT

Of reemergence into consciousness

It occurs too suddenly

An intensive care nurse calling my name from far across the anesthetic void.

Loudly, persistently she calls for me to come back in

I do not want to come back in.

When I open my eyes

I know something enormous has taken place

Yet I cannot think what

Vague and mixed and calm

With the sense of distant panic

I can easily ignore.

A handsome young Asian nurse looks familiar

So familiar I wonder if we had ever had doings.

I ask him if we had met before.

"Yes," he smiles, "I'm your assigned nurse; we've met every afternoon for the last week to talk for an hour. Short-term memory loss is an unfortunate side effect to electro convulsive therapy."

I was sorry not to have remembered him and not to have had the doings.

"The brain is a funny thing," he tells me.

4.

Edison's medicine – II

Of history long
Of dream-time sleep,
Left temporal spurts
Geometric leaps.

Mindless voices seething
Gripping dark despair,
Hallucinations light to moderate
Dashed hopes of hope unclear.

Secrets never knowing the true and exact
Sidestepping and truth,
Of solitary living
In naturally frenzied mind.

Holding on they slither
Sliding hither thither,
To hear strange music
Before a note is played.

I know that tears belong to others
Of unknown wounds,
Treachery of mind unhinged
Behind the caring smile.

Sliding along walls of safe corridors
With meds to make you half undone,
Meal upon endless meal
And how are you feeling.

The brain is conquered
Depths of turmoil hot ironed flat,
Abandoned to fend for itself
Into the un-living yet undead.

Of whence did I come
Of whence shall I go,
For exit there needs an okay doing fine
While screaming voices hide.

Choke back on oxygen fanning these flames
That stokes this furnace,
That fuse this sagging brain
I did not know it would be like this.

5.

Poor Thing

He no longer paints portraits
Or pretty pictures of vases.

Poor strangulated soul
Watching for his suicidal end.

He constructs large violent canvases now
Of murder and death torture and agony.

Sitting listening writing
Waiting for the moment to arrive.

6.

Here and There

I am with inpatient blottings not a happy camper
For each day is shot with nothing doing.

Now beyond depression sidestepping suicide
I sit and look and that is all.

I can stay in here or go in there
I can stand up or lay down.

I have mono silly arse' sis'
I can tell without being told.

I will write for my nurse a lovely ballad
Or if he prefers make a lovely salad.

Yet he is not fooled
For there is but cold comfort in a salad and a ballad.

When I become no longer, *"a danger to myself or others"*
I shall receive a certificate to say as much and leave.

7.

It

It came upon me at the age of fifteen in Austria.
However, when you get *it*
What then are you supposed to do with *it?*
Despite *it* you go about your day-to-day teenage life
You try to ignore *it*
But *it* will not ignore you
It can turn a mind crazy insane
Slam you up against the wall
Where a six-foot rainbow butterfly pushes through brick
For the shock value of *it* I suspect.

Sometimes I disremember me and *it.*
Some say this is schizophrenia
Manic-depressive-neurotic-self-harming-disorder
They give you pills and electric currents
You take *it* naked to the streets in rubber flipflops
Friends and relations turn from you and *it*
They want you and *it* gone so you go
You take *it* to San Francisco
Stay with *it* in the Haight/Ashbury
Where you and *it* might or might not even belong.

8.

Saul's Poem

Said the man in the maroon nylon dressing-gown

with the dangerous confiscated cord:

"Famous *poets*? Don't talk *famous* poets to me!

And I'll tell you something else for free . . .

Life-threatening craziness, that is what well-known poets cause in unknown
poets . . .

This is a fact I'm telling you, but not a well-known fact

Believe me, time and again am I a witness to this

Perhaps it's all professional resentment . . . all the same . . . But then what
do I know?

Do I look to you like a friend of famous poets?

Take my friend Saul, *please*, take my friend Saul!

May God give his blighted soul some peace!

A man you could only describe as an extremely unknown poet

Unknown? . . . No one could hope to be more unknown than Saul . . .

Very depressed he was, and here in America, suicidal.

A terrible lingual disadvantage Saul worked with . . . Hebrew and Yiddish
he had, some German, whatever . . . but English, not much to speak of.

Now, that woman poetess, Patti Smith, and Allen Ginsberg too, another
poetess . . . two well-known English-speaking writers of poetry.

And Saul, what? . . . a poor immigrant and not even made American yet and
some hopes there.

Now, this woman poetess, this Patti Smith, an American poetess-cum-singer

She wrote and she sang this long poem, a while back

About horses . . . something about horses . . .

Had horses in it anyway

This song, this horse poem, my friend Saul swore blind he thought about writing, in Yiddish, twenty-five-years ago

With this horse poem you might say, she beat him over the finishing line by a short neck, see?

She sort-of sang it too of course, loud, with music, which makes a lot of difference in a long poem

Lot of noise, guitars and drums to fatten out the words

Saul claimed in that one song, proved *she* had *his* genius

Poor Saul, he got very depressed over that horse poem

Even after I helped translate it with him into Yiddish

What can I tell you?

He loved that poem, yet he hated that poem . . .

Thought he might kill himself over it

A mad man or what, to kill yourself over a poem?

He wrote a long letter to that woman poetess, Patti Smith

To tell her you first needed remembering to be forgotten

He waited a year he waited, but he never heard back

Knowing Saul, he mailed it to the wrong address

In chronic depression, out of his mind Saul went . . .

I caught some of my own poetic depression from Saul

Saul, he died unknown, forgotten, with not even anything forgotten to forget."

9.

The Sadness of Mashed Potato in Gravy

With damaged-people greed
The once handsome man ingests his dinner
Slurping with such gusto
Spooning with such concentration
I watch and squirm for him.

I cannot look away
The mess around his toothless mouth
The grease upon his square stubbled chin
Face bent to the plate
Oh, the awfulness of mental malady.

Will I get like that?
Do we all get like that?
What utter sadness
Of damaged people eating
With mashed potato and gravy in their hair.

10.

Portrait of an Inmate

In dappled muted life
The inmate does not shine
But shares his shaded bed
With quiet desperation.

Tears through threshold image seep
Where mind and thought
Should never dwell
Where against all reason horrors slip and shove.

Love there once was to distraction
With sworn life laid down
Yet his face now scarcely remembered
Or even if he was circumcised or not.

Sights and sounds
Not one's own
And too much sleep not enough
And now only death will help this dying.

11.

Come to San Francisco and Go Mad

My semi-private roommate snored so loudly
I asked to sleep in the vacant padded cell
A windowless dead and quiet space
A mattress fixed to the centre of the floor.
The nurse said, "I don't see why not."
They chucked me out of my padded room one night
For a wild young man dragged in screaming
Needing tender restraints upon my warm mattress.

In the morning I sat with him at breakfast.
"When I drink," he said, "I lose my mind,
I just go shit-crazy."
He comes from Idaho.
"I'm a simple farm boy at heart," he said.
"You're a simple closet-case at heart," I did not say.
"A lot of people," he said, "they come to San Francisco to find them-
selves, right?"
"No," I said, "most come to lose themselves, and go crazy in the doing of."

I sat with him at lunch, "You're really wise," he said.
"No, not really," I said, "only a bit of a smart-arse."
Four weeks in San Francisco and he is lonely and homeless.
At dinner he suggests we might "team-up outside."

"Wow," I thought, "I need that like the holes I already have in my head."

Or maybe accept the mad challenge

For I see it already laid out before us

Two tender crazies without restraints on my warm mattress.

12.

Creeping Death

With the onset of age
Some expect to develop a mellow serenity
A certain wisdom
Where worldly cares melt away
Leaving one in a state of happy grace
With dignity and fortitude
A sense of subtle irony and humour
Ever ready to face one's natural end.

Well, I don't feel a bit that way
No, not even one bit
The mellow and the serenity elude me
Happiness grace and dignity avoid me
I will silently shout
Chaotic and mental
Cry and thrash
Not wanting quite to exit like this.

I can only wish to drift away quietly during a nap
Or gently at sunrise like a tubercular Victorian maiden
And why are these fucking drugs not working
In maintaining constant mental abstraction
Nibbling you to death cell by padded cell
Only thoughts infested and rank
Only their stench beating you down
Until your last unnatural gasp.

This is my no sleep three-in-the-morning reality

Waiting for someone to rescue me

Afraid to leave this room

Knowing what will happen

Seeing my legs buckle

Whacking my head

Sprawled across the sidewalk

I listen for the sun's rumbling rise and it is not pleasant.

13.

Semi-Private

Outside the loony-bin window of my semi-private room
A giant London plane tree stands looking in
As did the one outside my bedroom window in London
Watching and reminding me of our young love
On those grey chilly drizzly Maida Vale mornings.

One freezing wet morning
He held me warm in his thick branchlike arms
Would not let me get up and go to work
I struggled and laughed at first
He persisted and I got annoyed
I said I would lose my job
"Good!" he said
He held me in his tight embrace
I said he had no right to hold me against my will
He said he did not care
He would not let me leave when everything was so right
"So just shut up and kiss me."
I resigned myself to his romantic kidnapAnd would call work later with some lame excuse.

The loving memory caused my chest and eyes to ache
Made me long to escape California
Not right now some other time perhaps, but not like this
We should have stayed forever in that bed in Maida Vale
Tucked-up warm and kidnap snug in his arms

Not here in San Francisco with him long dead
Cold in his grave and me in this semi-private bed
With the watching London plane tree making no sense.

14.

Like Father Like Son

I have been queer and mad
For sixty-two years
And my father queer and mad
For sixty-two before me.

"Madness, it is not what it used to be," he might have said,
"And if mad long enough
Those brilliant flairs and desperate movements
Slack off and turn into pudding-headed repetition."

"And where the constructive madness in that?" I agree,
"One just grows old and dull and bloody boring.
You were quite right to have died at sixty-two."
And here I still sit muttering at birdies from a bench.

15.

Don't Talk to Me

"Don't talk to me about psychology,"
I told the psychiatrist.
"Don't talk to me about undiagnosed brain-conditions."

"I am," I suggested inanely attempting to attract the doctor's
attention, "an end in myself."
The doctor did not look up; doctors rarely look up.

"Don't ask me, why the tears.
If blubbing is what I need to do right now I'll blub.
There's no alternative, so I'll sit and blub a while."
"It's something like schizophrenia, but not that
Then something like a manic-depressive disorder, but not
Then something like epilepsy, but not that either
Something along those lines . . . or something
Perhaps I'm just having a lifelong nervous breakdown of some kind."

"No wonder," I muttered, "suicide is on the rise."
"*What?*" the taxi driver turned. "Do you want Kensal Rise, or
Brockley Rise?"
"I *said* Maida *Vale*, not *Rise*," I lied. "*Randolph Avenue.*"
"Right, mate," he snapped, "got it; you just sit back, and keep your wig on,
all right?"

"Don't talk to me about mental illness, mate" the taxi driver continued
rounding Marble Arch. "I got a metal plate in my head thanks to my stint

~ 21 ~

in the army. *Real* mental illness I'm talking about here; smashed skull and bits-of-brain-missing mental illness . . ."

"I told my doctor there is not a speck of serotonin in my entire body . . ."
I said, "And not an iota of melatonin in there either . . ."

"Don't talk to me," the taxi driver said, "about electric-shock treatment not being as primitive as it used to be . . ."

"Don't talk to me," I replied, "about modern techniques in convulsive therapy making the procedure safe and painless."

"No," laughed the taxi driver," don't ever talk to me about mental illness. I've enough trouble as it is; and what with my old mum . . . been bloody bonkers for donkey's she 'as."

"We have a lot in common not to talk about," I said.

"Yes, mate, we do, don't we?" the taxi driver replied.
Then he asked himself up for a cup of tea, and we had a bit of rough slap 'n' tickle on the bathroom and kitchen floors.

16.

Genes

Three of his brothers killed themselves
Whom my father often thought to follow
Son like father I too inclined that way.

We shared no love or hope
Yet curious as to what we might next think
Interested in ourselves and not much else.

Cancer killed him at sixty-two
Yet I might go on awhile perhaps
Just sit tight to see how death takes me.

17.

Four-Dimensional Being – Logic or Idiocy

Four-dimensional being realised in "full"-meditation.
In meditation *1. – (one.)* moves as *one.* in "space and time,"
But if *1.* allows for the constant state of change
1. will know that any *1. –* solid becomes simply energy –
That is energy of itself and not of the *1.*
So what *1.* knows is pure energy.
This energy of *1.* is a constant
It is never lost
It will never cease.

No material images
Thought or non-thought
Can serve to be four-dimension energy of motion –
Energy in all directions.
One is energy in a four-dimension continuum.
Once this is known to *1.* there can be limitless application,
Which in the human mind can result in total all-knowing bliss,
But also, total unknowing madness.
Once *1.* is known however,
1. cannot be unknown.
That is what I write here anyway.

18.

Of No Account

A poem a day
Some say
Will keep madness at bay
But I have mislaid my Wittgenstein wits
And do not know where to find them
I thought I left them in the kitchen
Or maybe by the bathroom sink
But no . . .

Now I hear your eminent husband
Wants my phone number
To lecture me
On "appropriate behavior"
Which coming from him
An ex-drug addict and ex-con
I would find immensely amusing
But do give him my number anyway.

So, about this madness a day
To keep poems away
I still have pills
Against the ills
Which cause me not to remember
What I was going to say
Or the name of old so-and-so
Whom I think I never much liked anyway.

Just tell them I have had a wonderful life

Or tell him I have had a wonderful life

Or keep it zipped and say nothing at all

And no last words rearranged for posterity

It all amounts to the same in the end

I cannot be drawn into futile discourse

Or self-justifying mode

Go fuck yourself but do so in silence.

19.

Hitler's Ball

♪Hitler, he only had one ball,
Hitler, he only had one ball,
His Muvver, she stole the other,
Now he hasn't, got any, at all . . .♪

♪I dreamed of Hitler with the nut-brown hair –
He was scarcely four feet tall
With the voice of a Mädchen
For he had no nuts at all . . .♪

"The most controversial human being
That ever lived," Hitler squeaked.
"Who," I asked, "*me?*"
"Nein!" Hitler screeched. "*Me*! Dummkopf!"

"I was a strict vegetarian, you know," Hitler mused.
I loved dogs and children . . . my lovely Nazi Empire."
"But did these qualities," I asked, "amount to much?"
"Yes, of course . . . they say I was most personable."

A new Nazi told me, "There are no swastika's flapping about
No pictures of Hitler hanging up, it is not like that anymore."
"No," I said, "old pictures of Hitler and swastika's flapping,
You now carry in other forms in your head."

In my dream Hitler and my father are twins

Two Austrians boys lovingly holding hands

Staring at me without expression

Their eyes glinting in the sky with diamonds.

20.

Men of Religion

I only like Mormons
Because they never say
"Screw you, asshole!"

I only like Jehovah Witnesses too
Because they never
Poop on your doorstep.

I only like Jews
Because you are not them
And beneath their contempt.

I only like Christians
I can slap
And who turn the other cheek.

I only like men of religion
That want me for sex
Fuck me good and give me cash.

21.

Remembrance

My grandmother was forty
Before she saw a black man,
My mother sixty
Before she saw a seahorse,
She thought they were fantasy creatures
Like mermaids and unicorns
My mother thought so too.

Boy, were they surprised
Both with their healthy outlooks on life,
How I shall always remember
My dear white-haired granny,
Parping in her fine old Gaelic tongue
Proclaiming, "*Oo, par-don em-warr, pigs.*"
Ah, those and these are the days and nights all right
And the nosh in this mental institution is not half bad.

22.

God of Tears

God remembered the earth
God looked down at his work
And God was sorely sad
Gabriel said, *"Buck up, God*
It's only the end of the world."

When wet falls from the sky
Rain or snow are assumed
But it on this day rained blood
The blood of the Lord
Lord God was bleeding.

God suffered
God saw mighty human stupidity
God saw human violence and greed
The distress grew too great for God
Until from God's eyes blood did pour forth.

"Please hang up and call 911," God heard
"Or go to your nearest hospital."
Gabriel took God in a Chariot of Fire
God arrived in the old nick of time
Gabriel told *The Daily Host*, *"It was just a cry for help."*

23.

Who Criminally Unwise?

He spent five years of his youth
In an institution for the criminally unwise
He said his father was a rich fat ugly homo lawyer
And his other father a rich fat ugly homo architect
And they had wanted a child together oh-so-much.
"*As-if,*" he said.

They mixed their sperm together
And paid a woman to have their baby
Even had breast milk delivered fresh
He alleged they habitually abused him
Fucked his head up
He hated them.
"Jesus," I said, "you ought to have them arrested."

"I can't," he said, "I killed them already."
"Oh," I said.
"The court still let me inherit though," he added. "A trust fund . . . I live off
the interest."
"You could write a book," I said, "then sell the film rights."
"Yeah, my lawyer," he said, "and his publicist boyfriend are dealing with
all that."

24.

Colin – "Brutally Stabbed to Death"
the Guardian headline read on Thursday April 15, 1999:

"*Detective Chief Inspector Richard Taber said: "This is one of the most horrific stabbings I have ever seen. It was particularly brutal and tragic. The discovery of the body must have been extremely distressing for the friend who found him.*"

I found my best friend my love my partner
His life hacked to shit on the kitchen floor.

They never found the knife that killed Colin
They say it corrodes in the Thames at Vauxhall.

They found the young man though
The one Colin propositioned in the kitchen.

And instead of saying, no thanks
He stabbed Colin to death.

I remember that steel kitchen knife well
It delivered an excellent cut.

Dazed by the not guilty of murder verdict
I went into the Clerk of the Court's office.

He asked sympathetically if I would like a cup of tea
No thanks, I said, all I want is the first flight out of here.

25.

Colin – London Incident

As I approached the suspiciously dark house
A sudden concern racked my gut
My nape hairs tingled when I opened the unlocked door
Inside a thick and palpable silence
I knew right then my friend was in there dead.

In the twilight he lay butchered upon the kitchen floor
His blood splattered across the walls and ceiling
I watched him in this raw tableau for a while
Then went to the front room to call the police.

Three months on:
The police said I could have the keys to the house
The cleaning team had been so everything was all right.

As I approached the house
I knew everything was not all right
I unlocked the front door to a thousand flies and choking putrid stench
The kitchen remained as I last saw it
Only now in bright sunlight minus my butchered friend
I looked and gagged at the scene for a while
Before going into the front room to call the police.

The police apologetic – a mix-up in directives
They would send in a clean-up team tomorrow
They would need they said to shut the house up again for at least a week

Or, it was tentatively suggested, I could clean it myself.

Pools of congealed stinking gore lay thick and still moist under the refrigerator and stove.

Blood splashed everywhere like an overdone horror movie

Blowfly maggots and disintegrated mould once fruit and bread

Closed windows opaque with fly droppings and foul vapour.

I went to the supermarket

Then spent four days alone in the house

Scrubbing and cleaning and rubbing my friend away.

One morning I stepped outside and locked the front door

Knowing any life in London now over

I slipped the keys through the letterbox and did not look back.

26.

Colin – What a Bloody Mess

The evening I found you hacked to death
All across the kitchen
I mumbled, "Jesus, Colin, what a bloody mess."

Months later standing there with the maggots
And stench
I exclaimed, "Jesus, what a bloody mess."

A few days before you were gutted
I cooked dinner using every pot we had
And you said, "Jesus, what a bloody mess."

If we could then but have known
Sensed what a Jesus bloody mess
It was really going to be.

27.

Colin – Murder of You – April 7th, 1999

The young man came named Dick
Slipping a length into my friend,
Ripping that so carefully balanced life
Right out of him.

His meat thwacked all about the floor
He is not my best friend anymore.

Black blood pooled and clotted
Splattered and sploshed.
Ah-me oh-my, across that new kitchen floor
Everywhere
Jack's son the Dripper Pollack-style.

Killed by the young man
He had often looked for
With a rigid eight inches thrust into him
In out in out
Again
Over and over
Seventeen times
Before their eyes glazed
And all was kingdom come.

I don't know why he did that
So sudden

So violent

Making you so completely gone forever.

Once you favoured reincarnation

But I told you that sucks

With all that better-luck-next-time crap.

In that horrific nightmare scene

I felt his stillness

His utter silent peace

It won't be long, I said

This is only a phase

Don't worry about it, dear,

Mostly life for most *is* bloody murder.

28.

Crown of Thorns

The wounds of Holy Jesus slammed upon me
While feeling Golden Delicious and Granny Smith in the supermarket
Overwhelmed in the frozen section
I closed my eyes and sat down for a moment.

Thought drunk or drugged they called the security guard
And "*Sir*, we are going to have to ask you to leave . . .
Sir, you need to get up *right now* and leave . . .
Leave *now*, or we are going to call the police . . ."

And the thorns spiked deep into my brain
And my face twisted ugly in grief and pain
I got up
I left the supermarket sick and humiliated.
The Jesus within once more forsaken.

XX. My Policeman Friend – Real-Time Politics

My policeman friend said,

"My buddy at the station, he told me last night about this top-secret governmental department memo involving sixteen billion dollars in research projects."

"Well," I said, "I guess that memo can't be too top-secret then, can it?"

"What? Why?"

"Well, if you and your buddy know about it, how top-secret is that?"

"Oh, well, we're trusted police officers . . . anyway, he said this independent company intends to gather together the entire population of dogs in the U.S . . . he hates dogs; and somehow simultaneously drop them from aeroplanes all over China at an altitude of no less than thirty-two thousand feet."

"Why?"

"I don't know it's top-secret; but he heard this plan is called "Action Dogs over China" or something like that, and it would instantly solve all the world's peace problems."

"How exactly?"

"He said they would be poison dogs, with rabies, or viruses or something."

"What, are they going to float them down in harnesses on little doggie parachutes, and why thirty-two thousand feet? They'll be frozen solid by the time they hit the ground."

"I don't know, maybe that's part of the plan, he didn't say, but the communists would eat the virus poisoned dogs . . . or get bitten."

"Then what?"

"I don't know, I told you, it's top-secret."

"I think you mean, top-stupid."

"No, he told me, and also Middle East terrorists, they have a similar plan called, "Pigs Over Israel" raining viral pigs down all over Israel."

"Pigs . . . wouldn't viral chickens be more appropriate; how many Israelis are going to be sitting around eating poisoned pigs?"

"No, I think Israel is probably more of a psychological country and would have adverse effects on the global equilibrium . . . or something like that he said anyway."

"I think, the both of you are bad insane policemen and should report one another to the authorities as such as soon as possible."

"No, well he can't be insane he's Latino and a really ace marksman, *and* he won another police bravery medal last year, *and* he's got a wife and six kids, so how insane could anyone like that be? *And* he's a Catholic too."

I looked at my big handsome policeman friend, and I did wonder.

30.

My Love My Toilet-Roll Holder

Mad and quick with his fists
Pete was tough and looked like a fighter
But he ought to have been a better fighter
For he often got well-biffed
Then he looked a pretty lousy fighter
Sprawled bloodied on the street.

I hate Pete now because he was killed
I hate him because I loved him
He died before I got to tell him
What a monster he was
What a wonderful fucked-up monster
What a beautiful piece of shit he was.

I want to tell Pete all those thing
And a lot more besides
I wanted to write them down
And read them back to him
Grab all the shitty words
And rub them in his face.

Just as well Pete's dad had him incinerated
Though I wouldn't have jumped up and down on his grave
I wouldn't really have cut off his balls to make a condom-bag
I would just have dug him up and given him a brush down
I would have washed him and kissed his face

I would have taken his mummified body home on the tube.

I would have sat Pete securely on a stool by the toilet
His two outheld index fingers positioned as a toilet-roll holder
If future inquisitive toilet user guests asked, I would say,
"Yes, well, of course having a lover is all very well and good
Though at best a sadly transitory, a temporary arrangement
Yet a lover as a functional toilet-roll holder lasts a lifetime."

31.

Mr. X

"In his last will,"
The lawyer said
"Mr. *X* left you a leg 'o sea."

For years Mr. *X* came to me
For massage sex and dinner
And always tipped me big.

He left me right and left
That I need not wobble and bend
Down Hello Sailor Alley.

"Stop with the sex and whacky life," said Mr. *X*
"Come find love and peace with me
In the Berkeley Hills."

I could not go just then or ever
For I wanted tiny Tom big Dick and Harry too
But thank you, Mr. *X* for the leg-up 'o sea.

32.

Trick Questions

"Do you love your mother?
Well, do you?

What of your father?
Do you love your father?

What of family or friends?
Do you love anyone?

Do you like anyone?
Do you like me?

What of yourself?
Do you like yourself?"

"I like animals
And sometimes I like art."

"Yes, well, yes, I suppose . . .
So, same time next Friday and have a nice weekend."

33.

Hermit Sanity

There is a hammock
Between two ancient oaks
And here I would live
By sun and moon
If I could.

I would live
In the air
With only the sound
Of the breeze
And a heartbeat.

34.

Strictly Art Illusion

Art does not accommodate orthodox living modes
There is no escape from anguish, pain or boredom in art

Art describes psychosis
Depression and mental imbalance

Art is not a tool for personal fulfilment and joy
No embodiment of happiness there

Art is not therapy, release or pleasure
Submit to the abhorrence and isolation

I move around with a paintbrush
Like someone with an illness

Outline my condition
Then colour it in

Destroy your art when completed
Or it becomes mere merchandise.

35.

Tip Big

Three to five -
"Come sit on my lap
And I'll give you a shiny new sixpence
There's a good boy
Shall I ride you to market upon my cock-horse?
Up we go
You like that don't you?
Yes, I can tell you do."

Six to eight -
"It's our secret so tell no one
Promise me now
Something very bad will happen if you tell
You don't want something bad to happen, do you?
They may well come and take you away
Tuck your shirt in and here's a half-crown
Off you go and remember what you promised
Our very special secret just you and me
No one else never, ever."

Nine -
"Be careful with those teeth now
Just hold the tip wet like that with your lips
Now use your tongue too
That's right back and forward like that
You know how I like it

See if you can fit it all in your mouth
There just like that
Beautiful wonderful . . .
Well, alright here's a ten-bob-note for you
Off you go . . . you avaricious little sod."

Ten -
"That's right
Open your legs a bit more
Let me feel your bum hole
There we are that's nice
Here I'll use a bit of spit
Feel how slippy and nice that is
Just one finger
There that doesn't hurt now does it
See how hard you've made me
See how nice that feels rubbed around your bum hole . . .
Well, here's your pound note . . . you bloody shameless whore."

Eleven to thirteen -
"Have naught to do with females
Nasty dirty smelly creatures
Put it in a girl and see what you get
Horrible diseases to make it turn black and drop off
Eve's curse women carry
We must love the naked body of Christ
The shape you can see through his sweaty loincloth
When I'm in you or your mouth on me
Think of the shape of Jesus stretched on the cross

Like a sacrament between us . . .

Here's your fiver . . . you mercenary little bastard."

Fourteen -

"Stop that whinging you're not a child

It doesn't have hurt that much

You're just being awkward . . .

Here, here's your damn ten quid extortion money

If you think it will make you feel any better about it."

When I looked up again, he was dead

Lucky for me, it was his heart they said

He just died all of a sudden it happens

Some terminal thing or other

Sex turned deadly

Sex killed him unto death right on the spot

I tipped myself with the sixty-eight pounds in his wallet.

36.

DRW 1957 – 1989

Towards the end he loathed me
Because I tested HIV negative
He despised me because I was not dying of AIDS.

Towards the end
I loathed going to see him
Because he was dying and I was not.

"I guess you call yourself a survivor," he sneered.
"Who the hell survives anything?" I asked
"And survives what exactly?"

"Though maybe unlike you," I did not say
"My rectum has not kept open-house
For the last decade."

I left his hospice room thinking
"Do yourself a favour and just die."
"You'll get yours!" he shouted after me.

"Hurling faeces at nurses," I told him
"Will get you no brownie points around here, mate."
It proved in fact the last mad straw.

"Why aren't you dead!" he bellowed.

"Die you cum-sucking faggot!" he screamed.
We all rather wanted him to get his skates on and depart.

His mother sobbed, "Please, dear God, heal him or take him."
But they took him back to Oregon instead
I felt unashamedly relieved.

His brother called
He said he had fought to the last
It had not been a good death.

"The virus turned his brain to mush," he said
"He went out kicking and yelling
"It was all pretty grim."

He was once a loving friend
And I shall
And will not miss him.

37.

Fun Time

I received a late-night phone call from a jilted love
Screaming how he was going to come over to my place
Cut out my shit-stabbing heart and shove it up my ass.

"Well Roger," I replied
"That does not sound like too much fun to me
But you know me, I will try anything once."

Still upset he screamed some more then hung up
He never did show up
Though I waited up for a full hour.

38.

Woe Ain't unto Me – 70's Style

"Yes, I know, I know I am articulate and amusing
But from the back does this intellect make my head look fat?"

"I am aware of my hard flat stomach and broad shoulders
Yet suffer so from physical and cerebral isolation."

"I am, yes, I am healthy tall and slim with nice fair hair
Though awash in major depression and suicidal ideation."

"You know I am good sex and generally give my whole
But my body and mind they run near empty."

"Yes, I am well read and travelled, I write and paint some
Though languid and the doings of art mostly pain me."

"I do, I have some income yet such a lot to bear
But you know me, never a one to complain."

"I simply observe and never react
Though given to addictions and perpetual cynicism."

"I am, I am oh-so, so weary . . ."
Oh, Beulah, be a love will you and peel me a grape."

39.

Go

1.

Curled in a bush
Or turned insane by neighbours
In the trap of rent-control.

Just over there
Within a few breaths
I will flip
Slip over the edge.

Give up give in
Mumble and crumble down
With no shame
No nothing.

Sunk in lunacy
The final letting go
Shouting falling screaming
Losing all control.

The pain never goes
Raw brain gutted mad
Incarcerated behind bars of safety
Where else to go?

2.

Going mad again

For there was nowhere left go

Thought of Israel

But knew

There was no escape.

Thought of Vienna

Father's home

Go seek a sense of him

He left too soon

Went to Cambridge.

At Cambridge

They said you must eat and rest

Thought of not going mad

But already was

Soon it will be time to go.

40.

This Perverted Life

When born
He craved only warm flesh and smiles
And a milky wet nipple.

At age one
He knew the silent bliss
Of life flowing within without.

At age two
He spoke with plants and sod and loved the mud
Whispering to the clouds and rain drops.

At three
He listened to the sun and the moon
Conversed with the unseen and sat in puddles.

Then from four
They sent him to learn perpetuation and participation
Shapes for dull but useful tools.

He forgot about the early truths
Yet his voices and visions remain
Though unable now to fully grasp their meaning.

Then with fingers of bliss and horror
He can only think to laugh or cry or die
Though sometimes the truth edges through.

We are traded in too young
Denied growth and blossoms of our own
For nothing but this myth and absurdity.

41.

Random Thinking in Custody

The hell of these people
They are not worth the cost
The wreckage of minds
With only the barred windows for escape
Only the sad and locked metal doors.

Genius or no I can always smell a loose screw when I see one
Deeply disturbing is abnormal psychology
Requiring occasional periods of institutionalisation
No prizes here for common-or-garden thought.

I was told once by my grandfather that twice
As a wee wain he drapped on my heed
On the flagstones in the hall
And how once I did a shit in his hat in that hall.

That handsome doctor
Contrives to test my intellect
In ways he finds wanting
It will not work
For he does not know
He is my reflection
I see him too clearly.

Mother was a woman
Her husband was a man

Their daughter was a woman too
Some uncle's name was Sam.
This uncle liked to use my lips
Played havoc with my bum
I did not like it very much
Infused in uncle's cum
"You will die and mummy too
if of this you tell."
But not until I reached fifteen
Did his ass get sent to hell . . .

My friend of old said, "I *know* that God does not exist
But I *believe* God exists."
I said, "I believed you *were* a moron
But now I know you *are* a moron."

He wiped his tears saying, "I wish I were dead."
I laughed and said, "Yes, I wish you were dead, too."
In such a to-do what can one do?
So we giggled and fucked like two monkeys in the zoo . . .

Another trainee wet-nose mental doctor looms
Expecting recall of a lifetime mental
For first-hand experience in mental
I think fucking not
All the same note-take and asking:
"So, what seems to be troubling you?"
Will I reply, "Ur, well, do you mean stuff like voices, visions, mania, torment and that sort of thing?"

"Yes. And anything else?"

Will I say, "Hmm, or do you mean things like excess sexual activity as
a prepubescent?"

"Yes. Anything else?"

"Or maybe you want more in the way of violent and manic-depressive step-
father abuse?"

"Yes. And is that all?"

"Or how about the suicidal mouthy young queer in London angle getting
himself punched-up or booted about?"

"That's right. Anything else?"

"Well, how about the dozens I knew who died horribly of AIDS . . . with
two assisted? Is that more the stuff you're after?"

"Yes. And?"

"Or would you enjoy hearing about finding my best friend hacked
to death?"

The wet trainee will stifle a yawn and look at his watch

"Well, is that it?"

The wet trainee will not find me uncooperative

For I pre-despise him and will not speak at all

Or maybe touch-him-up and risk the restraints . . .

42.

Queen Ester

Queen Ester
Queen of Scotland during a pre-primitive period
Came to me in my dream
Man, what a horrible great hag
Ester the fat, acid-tongued Queen of the radical triglyceride tribe.

She demanded to know why I slept
When there were mighty battles to fight and win
I told her, "Before I went to bed
I took some Vicodin, Ativan, Chloral Hydrate and Gabitril
So do not exactly feel like fighting battles right now."

"Ock, laddie!" said Ester. "Could you no spare a wee lassie a Vicodin
or two?"

"Pharmaceuticals," I replied, "were not around in the early triglycer-
ide period."

"I ken that, son," she said, "but ma healer's gang-awa' wi' the hip replace-
ment surgery, the noo."

"Oh, all right, but I am only giving you ten, okay?"

"Oh, that's lovely, son," Queen Ester sighed, "and saves me using my great
*claidheamh mór** on your wee heed."

(claidheamh mór* Gaelic. Clay'more – a Scottish two-edged broadsword.)

43.

Happy Together - 1996

We fly to Bueno Aries
Take the number 46 bus to La Boca
Check into a broken-down fleabag hotel
At 1617 Av. Don Pedro de Mendoza
Just look at us so happy together.

He gets works at *Bar Sur* a tango bar
Then at *Central* (Chinese) *Restaurant*
I fall in love with Lai Yiu-Fai
Though he is really Tony Chu-Wai Leung
Look at us now happy together

On our wrecked iron bed
There is bliss and heartbreak
Or a semblance thereof
He gets a job at a slaughterhouse
Now look at us still happy together.

He drives alone to the Iguazu Falls
Caetano Veloso sings *Cucurrucucu Paloma*
He gets sentimental and wet
Then goes home to Hong Kong
Don't look at us anymore.

44.

Cantankerousness Costs Nothing

An annoying young East Coaster sat next to me at the café
An arrogant up-start starting up a start-up
Bellowing at New York on his phone
He gripped a mighty bottle of California spring water
Loudly sipping
Sip, sip, sip
Sip, sip, sip
Every ten seconds
Sip, sip, sip
Sip, sip, sip
Ranting and sipping
Sip, sip, sip
Sip, sip, sip . . .

Ah, but with my erotic and petulant fantasy
I follow and accost the blighter in the toilet
Inserting his water bottle up his arse
Slipping his cell phone down his throat
Swathing cum sodden briefs about his head.
"*Don't leave me this way*," the song rings out
"No, please don't!" he tries to cry. "I may dehydrate."

In satisfied crazed wonderment I gaze at him next to me
This obnoxious insip . . . sip . . . sip . . . sipid young man.

45.

Soirée - 1975

I hold Thursday evening Soirées
Usually for one
Pablo and Gertrude
Are rarely seen
Joyce and Proust
Seldom appear
Hemmingway came once
But left straight away.

I don't care for I am self-arousing
And beyond all bearing
With enough *panache* for two
A bottle of rough red wine
And the economy size dildo will do
With lumps of Stilton and pineapple chunks
I am all fancy-nancy impaled on my cocktail stick
Though I am afraid Barbara Pym might pop in.

46.

Levi's Plaza Park

Near homeless in mind
And near mad in reality
I sank boneless to the grass.

"You can't sleep there," bellowed security
I did not know if to cry or to kill him
Either seemed plausible just then.

I looked at him and did not move
In my eyes perhaps he glimpsed the sadness or madness
And he turned and walked away.

47.

Selective Serotonin Reuptake Inhibitor Zombie

You have not fallen out of love with me
The Zoloft and Lexapro kicked-in is all
Working upon you this flat and flaccid indifference.

My own brain they fixed many a time
I know well that chemically lobotomized air
That I'm alright just for now Jack air.

It's tragic we are so fearful of life
We need such dulling
To experience any sense of peace.

Provoked and disturbed I will leave you now
Sitting on your couch
Gazing at your screen.

That is all and why are you crying
You're dumping me remember
A fine end indeed, goodbye, here's your key.

48.

The Edge

"Few psychiatrists," my psychiatrist said, "speak out against Electro
Convulsive Therapy

Although many have views against accepted norms."

While he spoke I looked at the bookcase behind his head

At his collection of replicas of old mechanical tin toys.
"In a survey from the American Psychiatric Association task force on ECT,"
he said

"Psychiatrists were asked, 'Is it likely that ECT produces slight or subtle
brain damage?'
41 percent voted yes and 26 percent voted no."

Some years

Sometimes for a month

On Monday Wednesday and Friday before dawn

They use electricity to rearrange my thinking

Afterwards life is soft and peaceful

I can watch things quietly for a long time

I am no longer forced to think much of the other things

Bad and useless thoughts diminish

I go about my business

I think I will never be the same again

And in a way I am not

But it is all right after a while

Eventually it is all right for a much longer while.

Yet I retain the thought that something is missing

The edge I cannot remember has been rounded off

Sometimes in a dream I glimpse that edge

And it is frightening and no good

Then I wake glad I am well convulsed

I think it better this way.

49.

Fine Art – 1969 & 1992

Ah, says you
Look and grasp
The miracle
The utter perfection
The wonder and sheer beauty
Of the human body
Ah, this body
This temple of the soul.

Urr, says I
And pretty unsightly temples they are too
These repulsive sausage skins
Bejewelled in nasty tussocks of hair
Packed with foul and stinking filth
These pulsating pus-bags
Oozing piss and shit
Saliva and bile
Blood sweat and snot
Tears and vomit
Squirting rank procreant flux
All slime and noxious gas
These our precious human bodies.

Addendum – 1992
If not from cancer you were long dead now
I would say come with me

Come view my many dying friends

This one a dark and handsome chap

Two-hundred and twenty-pounds of muscle

See how a plague year whittles him down

Blind and deaf a skeletal wreck as you became

Tell me now about the beauty of the human body

These fine temples of the soul

We remain but carcasses.

Last week Francis Bacon died

A wonderful rotting carcass of Francis Bacon horror.

50.

A Kindness - 1983

"Assist you to do what?
You have the balls to ask me?"

God, he is such an arsehole
I should hang up tell him to bugger off.

He dumped me for, "A man I'm in love with."
And for some born-again nonsense.

"Ask your lover or your beneficent God
To lend a helping hand."

It appears with this new quick-kill disease
The God and the lover are no more.

From the unbearable pain and weeping sores
He asks me to help deliver him.

"Careful," a voice whispered
"Approach this with good grace or not at all."

51.

Stiff Upper

In my wavy mind I see you
As you were before the exodus

Though if you walked in right now
What would I do?

Fall to my knees
And weep at your feet

Claw your trousers off
Beg for what you do so well

Tear your eyes from your head
Rip your tongue from your mouth

Smash your brain in
With a blunt instrument

Contrive indifference
Blanked faced and cool

Smile with pretend friendliness
Convincingly ask how are you

Nice to see you

Let's do lunch sometime

The conscious choice of reaction
Seems unlimited

But prudence of course
Will rule the day

I therefore blink
And make you walk away.

52.

Sulks

On admission that aggressive hospital security guard
He went and confiscated my twelve-inch
Gutting knife boo-hoo!

That bloody bastard
I only had the knife a week
Never even got to use it.

I do think him mean
With his wonderous taut rounded belly
Crying out for a bloody good gutting.

53.

Cat Got My Brain

Early morning
God's bad voices are upon me
Warning
Advising
Coercing
Directing
Demanding
I cannot speak . . .

God's good voices say:
"Don't panic."
"Go with the flow"
"Adapt"
"Let it go"
"Keep busy"
"It's okay"
"You're all right"
"There is nothing wrong . . ."

I know
Listening to head voices
Is dangerous nonsense.

Yet they will speak
I will hear
My head aches with them . . .

Last week after cutting cancer from my talking head

I developed traumatic alopecia

They said it may grow back . . .

Life is disgusting

You wish yourself dead

But already inhabiting hell

You think well what's the diff . . .?

Neither passive

Nor disinterested

Only sleepless and worn out . . .

Here it comes again

And there it goes

Deep circles of light fluctuating out there somewhere

Out of right field beyond left temporal lobe

Tiny moments of brilliant madness

Commanding inconceivable sights and words

An alien brain inserted to eat me alive

I cannot stop it . . .

Rather sooner than later

They suspect premature snuffing in the offing

If something soon not done

Can't do coffee on Monday

I'll be at UCSF Langley Porter for the week

Zap the grey-matter

Then see what we shall see
Or not as the brain may be . . .

Thinking it sex play or fun I suppose
The yob I took home from Café Thug
Slapped me round the side of the head
I smacked the great galoot across the mouth
Making his eyes pour tears
Manfully he sniffed, "I'm not crying . . ."

At some point a nurse came in and said:
"The best things in life are not things."
I snickered, "Been at them fortune cookies again ah?"

Easy for her to say
She has every damn thing she wants
Or so she says.

She told me already about her new house and car
Her incredible big flat screen and small round husband
Her delightful six-slice bagel-toaster and the two kids . . .

You-big-lug-you
After my heart you are, are you?
You'll find no heart up there
Try take a look and see
Your iron clad slam-rod might do the trick though
Firm against the wonderous mighty man-clit
No need to appear in muse form for me

What trash you speak

You have no heart

You are such a freak . . .

Mr. Muse, do not try to get my goat

For my goat is not so easily got

And goats will devour almost anything

I shall call you Billy or Goat Shnookums

Sweet Shnookums if I will

Or I may call you my bitch-whore

Or anything I please

Stand there against the wall

Do exactly as I say

Press your aroused asshole against the weeping wall

And if you can take it you'll get it good and proper . . .

"Chris, man," I cautioned, "don't ride your skateboard crazy like that or
you'll be dead on it."

"What," he laughed, "you're the gypsy with the crystal balls?"

I watched him twirl and pivot away into the Stockton Tunnel.

Ringed and crossed with silver

I am the gypsy with tight crystal bollocks

Riding crazy did kill him

Over on Divisadero.

Thinking of Chris

The phone rang

He said he was coming over.

Careless minded crystal bollocks
Bending Chris shapes where they no longer bend
"No condoms," Chris said, "I hate those fucking things."

In some affected voice of an antique English thespian
A fellow, a patient fellow in looney land here asked
What I thought were the two best movies of the 90's
Why he asked I had not a clue.

I told him the two best films were from 1997
Happy Together by Wong Kar-Wai
And *Romy and Michele's High School Reunion*
Two positive unequivocal masterpieces
He had never heard of either he pulled an ugly face
"*Whatever*," he sniffed and turned away.

Another chap in the dull day room said
A poem should be effortless and free
Quick and to the point
Like a Leonardo drawing
Like a Mozart sonata
And shit like that . . .

In London that time
Dragging around the vacuum cleaner
I threw it at his head
I did not expect to find him
Screwing in my bed
On the bed would have been okay

But not in newly washed sheets

With some yob from Slough

With stinking crusty feet . . .

Reeling out more headcheese as we went

They wheeled me along for a final ECT session

But waking from the anaesthesia

I became unreeled and vaguely stoned for a week

Fighting hard not to gaze into the void too long

Trying to remember this something or other

Trying to remember the jumble

Stuff I thought I knew all of my life

But not and then some

Cat got my brain for sure this time . . .

Mind at rest

But never still

Never quiet.

Is sublimity a word?

Sublimity of mind in virtual death

Is all one requires

Is that it?

54.

A Hook in Time

A simmering need to use a cord
A hook upon the bathroom door.

There is nothing here for you
In this un-silent life.

Noose to hook is simply done
Quick go down and sink upon.

55.

Fourteen Tasks of Hercules

Settled in the loony day room

For a bit of daily group therapy

The group leader hands around this list

Of naive and impossibly helpful

Herculean tasks:

1. Activity
2. Talking to someone
3. Knowing your limits
4. Eating a well-balanced diet
5. Exercising regularly
6. Sleeping adequately
7. Making lists
8. Crying
9. Meditating
10. Taking time out
11. Creating a quiet scene
12. Listening to music
13. Making time for fun
14. Limiting stress

Oh, *please*!

Come on, already!

Let's be reasonable adult loonies here.

Then for a dreadful moment

I thought I might utilise

Quite dramatically #8

But quickly realizing #14

I bravely utilized #'s 1, 3, and 10

And flew to my room for a spot of #6.

56.

Madness, Mercy and Moisturisers

Come to bed or I will kill you
Kill you so dead
I will eat you
Eat you so raw
I will eat you dry
So dry you shall cry out for my suck-you-lent moisturisers
Oh stop oh stop you will cry
I shall not stop.

Do not ramble across my face
In my ears
In my brain
I do not like you out-of-bed
Never did
Never will.

You make me ill with your bad goodwill
I would rather you sit on my face
And twirl
And twirl
To cause my tongue and hair to curl
You are of little worth except in bed.

Your out-of-bed values
Are not my out-of-bed values,
Therefore

We need do one for the another

You must do for me

Before

I do you in.

57.

Be Cautious

Be cautious when writing or talking in madness
It isolates and can send you raving to the streets
Instantly boring yourself and everyone else.

Vying to exist amongst other loonies and the destitute
Hemmed between the bourgeoisie and bulky security
Here we have created the thin edge of our wedge.

When mind and money dwindle too far
Driven to take or beg subsistence
No one lasts long on the streets.

58

XXI. My Policeman Friend – Not my Sanity

My policeman friend said,

"I don't think you really love me anymore, do you?"

"I do love you . . . there are so many things about you that I love."

"Well, you have a funny way of showing it then."

"I only I wish I could love you in the way you want me to love you."

"You could adapt to living in the suburbs, if you really wanted to."

"It's not just the suburbs; I wish I could just sit here with you on your couch in your house and be thoroughly content and happy to be here with you, and happy to be practically married to you."

"But you can't, you don't want us to be life-partners, and so you want out, and so you don't love me anymore."

"I honestly wish I could enjoy watching cable television, having barbecues and drinking beer."

"You are, you're going to leave me, aren't you?"

"Sexually, aren't we great together? I love having sex with you."

"Even so, you're leaving me though . . ."

"Don't cry, please don't cry . . . "

"I love you so much; I think you will break my heart."

"I wish I could like all the things you like; the sports and the sit-coms and the news, or your music, or want to eat three meals a day, or go hunting and fishing with you."

"You said you loved me once."

"I still love you, and I wish I could live happily here with you forever . . . or until one of us bursts something vital and dies right here painlessly and in a second on the couch."

"Can't you try and love me more; come and live with me and we can try."

"Is this your wish for us, for our sane life together?"

"Yes, it is . . . what's wrong with it?"

"Oh, my dear man, I do love you, but I think your sanity is not my sanity."

"Please just try, say just for a year, or even six months? Come and live with me, and try? Please, just try."

59.

Vision and Madness – I
Before the fall

With such infinite weariness

When the beautiful lights appear beyond the bed

And once more possible

For a while

To choose to stay

Or enter a sleepy void

Directed by light

Drifting

Rocked gently back and forth

In a singular tranquil state.

60.

Vision and Madness – II
The falling

The next night or perhaps the same
Consciousness and sleep
Arise as one
And traveling within that state
As smooth as stepping from path to grass
Seen as is and has been
Came as no surprise which surprised me
And the insistent sparkling lights
Holding and supporting
With the murmur of numerous tiny voices
Far away from inside someone's ear.

61.

Vision and Madness – III

Mind taking off

Flying away

For a moment

For an hour

Then a spark

Existence returned

Blissful radiance

Shimmering colours.

If this be madness give me more.

62.

Vision and Madness – IV

Seen in a moment
All conscious and unconscious thought
That ever were within and without the universe
Every word or utterance ever voiced remains
All concepts unimaginable imagined
In the consciousness of all things
Open before me
If needed
If wanted
Any reaching hand may take it.

63.

Vision and Madness – V

I asked the doctor why

But he could not say

Do not seek knowledge of the self

There is no knowledge

No question no answer

Perceive oneself of oneself

I lay on the bed using what I do not know

Where only stagnation and death can arise

Here I need to endure for myself in the universe

No purpose in moulding and transforming mind

Into what I already know it not to be.

64.

Vision and Madness – VI

The mice of Langley Porter

Beautiful glowing hearts

Of single specks of dust

Floating in the room.

Infinitely wonderful molecular movements

In the structure of a tiny lice

Burrowing its way into the skin

On the belly of a *Wee, sleekit, cow'rin, tim'rous beastie*

Starting *awa sae hasty*

Behind the wainscoting near the bed

Wi' bickering brattle!

"Mice and lice in a hospital?" I ask.

"Mice *and* lice!

Mighty mouse served on a bed of lice!

Louty louse on Minnie Mouse!

Licensed mice with lice!

Minnie Lice with . . ."

"*Hey!*" a night attendant called, "keep it down, *Okay?*"

"*Okay!*" I called back, "Okay! *Okay!* Okay! *Okay!*"

Am I gone now socially unacceptable mad?

65.

Vision and Madness – VII

Guide the senses
To respond to reason only
Nothing else will do
Reinterpret correctly
That which is perceived
Previously mad
Disjointed thinking
Do this for you
No one can obstruct you
This process
Turn the mind to anything you choose
The necessary tools are at hand
Never before used
Become adept at handling them
Be master of your own mind
Your own happiness
Or go mad and perish.

66.

Vision and Madness – VIII

I see my crotchety genius father

A tiny glimpse

Amongst the wisest and the most holy of people

That have ever existed

Or will ever exist

Blank faces and their blank minds

Their personal enlightenments and intellects of no account

As the many millions of them struggle

To keep balance

On the back of a fine common jumping-flea

Quivering somewhere near

Over by the light of the half open door.

67.

Vision and Madness – IX

I understand correction is needed

A more determined non-effort

I will not do as they say

To think less of myself and condition

I will not think more or less of myself

I will think only of myself

Consume myself in self-interest

We cannot live in the reason of other people

I will live for myself

Alone in freedom

I owe nothing to anyone

No one owes me.

68.

Vision and Madness – X

The room awash

In crimson and orange light

A warm thickness flowing through the head

Running down along the spine

Dropping deep between a pair of parted legs

"Oh!" they exclaim.

"Is it gentle rape?" they ask.

"Is it violent birth?"

"Invaded by the penetrating tentacles of a space alien?"

"Penetrated by a deep thrust; the very long arm of the law?"

No, there are no more secrets here

No secrets anymore

Nothing need be kept hidden

"Yes, that's it; open your legs wide now."

And all will be revealed.

"There, there it goes."

"That didn't hurt too much, did it," stated the nurse.

Vulnerable?

Coerced?

Exposed?

Defiled?

Humiliated?

Liberated?

What?

69.

Vision and Madness – XI

Every cell in the brain
Every cell throughout the entire body
Falling into exact alignment
Slotted into place in complete harmony
With all there was
And was not
In all dimensions of all universes
Very grand
No great spiritual awakening this
No soul-expanding enlightenment here
Just guileless recognition
Once known naturally
Basic, fundamental
Natural, instinctive
Distant ancestors understood
Throbbing away in the primordial soup
But simple knowledge
Eroded
Pushed aside
In the painful struggle
Towards the final end
Of human presence.

70.

Vision and Madness – XII

There have been doctors
Looking at me
Touching me
In me
On me
Speaking about me to me.

The following day or the day before that
Someone wheeled me somewhere
With those bright halos of ear-splitting light
And a masked smile
Not just anyone's smile
But the smile
In realisation of everything
And anything
There had ever been
Or ever will be
In non-time and space
And you could balance the lot
Many trillions of times over
On the tip of a . . .
Microcosm within a microcosm
Blown away on a whim
"Count backwards from ten," he said
"Ten, nine . . ."

71.

Vision and Madness – XIII

A great shout of joy
At the recognition of all
A great laugh returned
Across the abyss
All happiness and lovely laughter.

72.

Vision and Madness – XIV

"Hello, in there! It's three in the morning," a gruff attendant advised.

"What?"

"Try and not talk and go back to sleep."

"Must I? Why?"

"Do you want something to help you sleep?"

"Yes, okay. I think a baseball bat smashed across my forehead might be nice?"

"Well, I was thinking more along the lines of a warm drink; chocolate or milk? Or whore licks."

"A whore's lick?"

"What?"

"What?"

"Horlicks."

73.

Vision and Madness – XV

I had fallen asleep

Lying awake in the void

Far above the bed

No physical body

Being of the ether

Feeling the earth move

Then back on the bed

Being of the bed

Being of the earth

As a child in mud

All shimmering warmth

Laughter inside and out.

74.

Vision and Madness – XVI

The day after that perhaps

Settling down

Looking (up) at the ceiling

Old fears return

The beautiful lights fade

Eventually extinguished

As the body

And mind

And the terrible

Simpering

Damaged ego

Claim theirs again.

An attendant before me sets a cheeseburger

He looks at me

I look at him

We look at the cheeseburger.

It is all over

Once you see

You can never again un-see.

75.

Vision and Madness Reprise

drug induced state?

a fit?

dream?

a natural state?

illness

distant talk

dura mater

arachnoid

pia mater

viral meningitis

cause not known

epilepsy

temporal lobe

just outcome

white bed

no feeling

war rages

across the surface of the brain

down the spinal cord

unwilling to move

brain and mind

moment by moment

mysterious changes

irrevocably altered

extreme grogginess

half sleep

silent dead people about the bed

"Thank you for coming."

"No meatloaf, thank you."

"Eat the vegetables."

now I must go

they vanish

great relief

they are dead after all

left alone

happy at their departure

another notebook inevitably

irrevocably burned

brain meds

people images

thoughts rambling

full fathom five

thy father in dirt

so much flotsam

dismissed from life

without permission

goodbye

no longer needed

what was needed?

air and water

"No lasagne, thank you."

"Well just eat some vegetables."

love cleared away

flick of a switch

ding-dong

ding-dong bell

loves-of-one's-life

not significant

deep sleep

nurse holds a box of milk

"Here drink some of this."

propped against pillows

hot head cold feet

something new

the nurse does not notice

seen either way

hot or cold

ends of the same condition

ultimately knowable

reach out and take it

such weariness

inside the head

the meds

impossible to tell

awake asleep

pleasant unpleasant

light of beauty

a decision to make

awake or void

drifting between tranquil states

but no separate state at all

only one

from one to one other

stepping from path to grass

"You're dehydrated

drink this."

awake asleep

awake asleep

awake asleep

no recognition

acceptance clear

sparkling light

insistent

holding everything up

Murmuring of tiny voices

far away

inside the ear

mind flying off alone

for a moment

then a spark

blissful radiance

shimmering colour

in a moment

all utterance

ever to occur

all conscious philosophy

all unconscious thought

within space and time

there to be heard

all concept imaginable

in physical life

in awareness

if needed or wanted

a hand reaches out to discover

doctors and experts

no satisfactory answer

knowledge gained

by oneself for oneself

"Eat some toast then."

"Eat some scrambled egg."

learn of brain malfunction

confronted in future

no doctors

no therapists

no pharmaceuticals

delve beyond the known

perceive oneself

use what one is

your own work of art

transformed mind

as only you know it to be

glowing heart in single speck of floating dust

infinite molecular movement in the structure of a louse burrowing into the skin on the belly of a mouse

moving along behind the wainscoting near the bed

mice and lice in a hospital

senses trained

respond to reason

reinterpretation of the perceived

no mad

disjointed thinking

for yourself

no one else

fully functional

mind turns to anything

tools at hand

but you can still go fuck yourself

applied logically

adept or useful

master of your own mind

your own happiness

enslaved

imprisoned from infancy

twist the mind to suit

in the name of love

in the name of God

of goodness

of convenience

glimpsing the wise and holy

that ever existed

will ever exist

blank faces

blank minds

personal enlightenment

voices of no account

millions struggle

balance

on the back of that common jumping-flea

quivering somewhere near

over by the light of the half-closed door

mice in a hospital

fleas in a hospital

seen in a moment

something wrong

determined effort

do not as they say

do not think less of yourself

your condition

think for yourself

think only of yourself

consumed in self-interest

live for yourself

"You don't want the cheeseburger?"

continue to do so

owe nothing

owed nothing

crimson light

warm flowing pain

along a spine

dropping deep

parted legs

gentle rape

violent birth

testicles and tentacles of an alien

"He's from the Middle East, I think."

penetrate

no secrets

nothing hidden

legs held open

as far as they will go

all is revealed

there

it doesn't hurt

vulnerable

exposed

coerced

defiled

humiliated

"Eat the vegetables."

raped

exact alignment

every braincell

slots into place

complete harmony

with all there was

was not

in all dimensions

in all universes

love

loving your mother

loving the love

no spiritual awakening

no soul-swelling enlightenment

once innately known

basic

fundamental

natural

instinctive

distant ancestors knew

throbbing in primordial soup

simple

basic data eroded

pushed gradually aside

in painful evolution

doctors looking

touching

talking

moving

nurses whispering

attendants calling

illness

stillness

chattering teeth

a rattle

tubes in nose

mouth

arms

penis

burning holes

burning halos

saturating light

the smile

the realisation

all that has existed

or will exist

"Try a little oatmeal."

balanced billions of times over

on the point of a needle

microcosm within microcosm

blown away

on a whim

great shout of joy

at the recognition

the great laugh

returned across the abyss

only happiness

only laughter remains

the attendant says

"Hello, it's three in the morning."

Something to help you sleep?

"No more meds, thanks."

"I meant a warm drink,"

he smiles, "chocolate or we even have Horlicks

This cheeseburger, I'll just stick it in the microwave."

imitation of life and . . .

"Oh, and there's ice-cream too."

76.

Pity

I do not recall much of middle age
But remember my young self clearly.

Perhaps old age I will not recall
But when would that be exactly?

"Pitiable old queer."
A young queer mumbled at me on the crowded tube.

"It's *schitts* like *you* I pity," I responded loudly.
I would have poked him had I a stick.

"You're only here through the slops of some *fuck*,
So don't hold yourself so grand, *Lovey*?" I told him.

His face turned beet red and disfigured with a sneer
And I would happily have poked his leg once more.

When old man contagions
Besmirch the body
And brain cells droop the mind
Then perhaps I won't mind a soupçon of pity and shtick.

77.

Five Ages of *Fuck Off!*

Diddled from three to fourteen
He grew up kind-of angry moody mad
But only cried in private
They said, "You'll become a wonderful artist."
In his head he said, "*Fuck off.*"

He stole and went to art college
From fifteen to twenty-five
Had sex with men for money
One john said, "I love you, so *very* much"
"In which case," he replied, "you can *fuck well off.*"

He travelled and went more mad
Between twenty-five and thirty-five
He buggered off to California
In time to watch the faggot's die
"Yeah, and they got *fucked right off.*"

He worked with books
From thirty-five and forty-five
Fixed sold and wrote the bastards
But sent sod-all to publishers
Never received the, "Thank you, but *fuck off.*" slip.

Forty-five and on
He has nothing to stop him now

For larks he might stalk and slaughter superstar artists

Pickle their sorry asses . . .

Or he might say, "You can all just, *fuck off!*"

78.

It's the Eggs is What Done Him In

All weekend they were hatching in his head
And on Monday he went mad again
I don't know why he just cracked
In madness he is very quiet you would hardly know
Hardly rocks the show at all.

I told him we have everything here in San Francisco
We have fog and sunshine and memories of other places
"I saw Jack and Sarah go up Russian Hill," he said
"To fetch a pail of poetry
But Jack fell down the other side and Sarah went tumbling after."

He said, "I really need to get more eggs."
Then he went and jumped off the Golden Gate Bridge
I don't know why, we had plenty of eggs
Perhaps he was overly depressed
Or just tired of the never-ending eggs.

79.

Sand and Ashes

The Bible may say
'The son of man hath nowhere to lay his head.'
Yet his fat sweaty arse
He parks just about any old place.

I remember our love naked in the desert
How the Sun burned us with kisses
When we showed too long God's Son
The place where the Sun never shone – *Ouch! It hurt so good*

Ah, our youth you said
I am more depressed than you
And to prove it committed bloody suicide
Now I hardly remember his face.

80.

Bay Area Living

He watched the man do the bouncy Zuckerberg Prance
The man with 100 billion dollars shoved down his pants
While others rushed to prance with billions well tucked.

After paying this month's rent
He will have $8.63 to live on
He lays still on the floor well fucked.

In London they used to shout, "Eat the bloody Rich!"
He sees soon enough will be quite enough
And Zuckerberg ass-tips skewered upon his bed of rice.

He pretends hunger is fasting
Pretends despondency meditation
For these are surely good things – what a joke.

The night streets are calling his name
Unlit doorways await his presence
And to arrive there takes but a moment.

81.

Reason Verses Bad Circuitry

The Contradictory
When you strive for a life of understanding and reason
Though challenged at every turn
By distorted and illogical visions
In all your mental beggary and buggery.

The Unpredictable
The circuitry when cock-eyed
Too loud too bright too extreme
All medication wrong
Too strong too weak too extra extreme.

The Arbitrary
Temporal lobe folly
Verses pro-reason
Pro-man verses conditional awareness
Pro-life verses suicide.

The Faked
It is all askew
There should be unconsciousness
Or fast running
Or face-off in the loony-bin.

The Hidden
The need for selfishness

Existing for one's own sake
Belonging to no one
No one belonging to you.

The Irrational
More attempts to communicate
From private hell
Trying to maintain a grip
In the throes of not-quite-right-at-all.

The Incomprehensible
To love a human being
Even when you know they are irrational
With scarcely a mind of their own
Wasted lives lived saturated in emotion and sentiment.

82.

Speaking With the Pigeons

"Listen up now, you pigeon people
At this wisdom here mislaid
From we, the mislaid tribe of Scottish Jews
May you well ask, such as
Such as, never shoving your haggis up a shofar
For this can lead to bad feelings
And possibly a nasty rash.

To thy wee wise mammies listen
Then do what thou wilt at thy peril
A wise wee mammie may say,
"Tight socks will slowly kill a man
I knew a man once wore tight socks
(Your father's father it was)
And look at him
An iron doornail not as dead."

For the young
Misery and madness
In their season
In the old
Misery and madness
For good reason . . .

He used to be
So gay and sprightly

He never pissed
Five times nightly
Now he has a tube bag and ball
And never has to piss at all . . .

"Ye ken something, son
From the moment we met
I never took to thee awfee much
Dini ask me why
And dini take it personal
For I dini take to many a soul
Know tis other folk doth cause the bane."

I told my nice Jewish doctor, "I need a facelift."
He tutted. "You do not need a facelift
What you do need is psycho analysis
Or maybe more electro convulsive therapy."
To decide we played rock/paper/scissors . . .

No, it is not just you
I see you too clearly
And it makes me sick . . .
And why am I
Conversing here with you apathetic birds . . .

He says he loves me
But I know he does not love me
I know he often does not even like me
I must tell him to drop the love stuff

Tell him the sex is great so let's just go with that, okay?
Brought up on a terrible dict of sentiment and emotion
Reason and consistency clearly never on his menu.

Oh well it hardly matters
While reflecting on one's mode of exit
From the here and now
Deciding life and death a matched pair
Or existing not at all
A happy nothing on which to reflect
Or if one favours a God, heaven, and hell
All quite nice too
One can but imagine
And I don't mind on my jacket pigeon faeces
When safely rocked in the arms of Jeesis . . .

XXVI
You think vile bricks
Yet shit kind words.

XXVIII
Eyes turned within
Despair to observe
No need to turn again.

He asked, "You get cold sores, don't you?"
"Sometimes," I said.
"That means you'll probably die from Alzheimer's disease."
"Possibly."

"I don't think I want a lover who'll get Alzheimer's."

"Oh, okay."

"You don't mind then?"

"Don't mind what?"

"Us not being lovers anymore?"

"Ur, no . . . but, you are, *who* again exactly?"

In London I asked the Pigeon Lady

"Aren't you the Pigeon Lady?"

The Pigeon Lady replied

"No, I ain't the *fucking pigeon lady*

I just feed the bastards is all."

"Well, you make them happy anyway."

"Pigeons don't know nuffin 'bout 'appiness

And only make them miserable if they did

Make 'em stark staring bonkers thinking like that it would

That's a big mistake making comments like that

Consider the fucking pigeons, mate, and learn something

An' all else is just a sack of tender loving bollocks."

You whom I once loved

I cannot imagine

You disgust me now

Like loud trumpet noise . . .

You know, I like to think myself something other than

"You sullen-lanky-streak-of-faggot-piss!"

Now nagging doubts asway me . . .

"No, no

Madness

It is not enough

Go way beyond the madness

But do not cry

If you should cry now

You would weep

Sob

Wail

Then you would scream

And never stop . . ."

Sadly, I know my comforting pigeon companions

Once this bag of victuals is replete

Whence I know shall fly the hell away

Abandoning me limp-bagged and bench-bound

And quite alone and quite right . . .

83.

Fac Ut Vivas
(get a life)

Slaughtered genius
Rotten within
Pushing hard
To feel the meat of my father's head
Absorbed beneath six feet of dirt.

Mind and heart break apart
But do I care
Why should I care
Lazy and needy misanthrope
A sad pair.

A mind endless in flashing images
Fortunate in painting
Ten thousand thought one complete
One small idea at a time
To work on for weeks months years.

A pen fast moving
In a hurricane's eye
Smooth across the paper
Before down-pouring crap
Where one tiny clinker may glimmer.

Dreams of killing flying carnage below
Yet where the blasted heath in California
No more of England, *please*
No stiff upper lips or gunboats
No more cream teas and guts of beer.

"You shall have," the council say, *"a generous thirty full days*
To get your act together
If after that period, you have not become socially acceptable
A useful member of society you shall needs be eliminated
Go and acquire some substantial mental grooming
Good luck and we shall see you back here in one month."

When real reality is confronted
Nothing can be the same again
Voices and visions continue to amaze
I am the John of fucking Arc
Of Nob Hill and fuck-in Chinatown.

84.

Resolve

Assiduously attend
When the demons and shadowy figures are upon you
For they will pull at great chunks of your mind
Stick long sharp needles into your brain
Delve deep to make you listen hard
To make you soft to scream aloud
In resolve you need prodigious strength.

Do Not Panic.
No, never panic
In panic you are lost
Watch and wait
Do not to let them push you into easy felo-de-se.

It may just be worth it.
Do not cry out
Do not call for help
Do not open your mouth or make a sound
You must remain still and mute
Voiceless as an anchorite
Silent as the monastic.

Speak to no one
Wait and listen
Only in silence will you save yourself
Listen for you might eventually hear

Then shall you rise up and soar through the vastness.

85.

Again Dream

You die again
In my dreams
You die again
And then again.

You are no longer
Alive with me
But your remains remain
In an urn with me.

Die again
And again
Just one more time
And your arse I'll bed for good.

Done with dreams
I scatter you
To the wind
Across the Tor.

86.

Zap Me

At 4:00 a.m. the distant phone rings
And I know it is time
A kind nurse appears
He wheels me to the room where they wait.

Here the kind anaesthetist injects me with:
Propofol
Methohexital
Thiopental
Thymatron
Remifentanil
Domitor
Etomidate . . .

Then the kind doctor electro convulses my brain
I do not feel a thing
I hope I never shall again

They are all so very kind.

87.

Leave Me Alone

I do not want to draw trauma
Paint it
Write it
Think it
Feel it.

I do not want drugs
Electrodes
Counselling
Therapy
I need to just leave myself alone.

88.

Murder Plan

My mind does not allow me ease at his slaughtered body
Affixing itself and carcass well in place
The world witnessed through 20/20 death-ray specs.

I dream of the murders I am yet not to commit.

Would an eye for an eye help erase this clarity?
If I found him out and butchered him
Roll dog-like upon his squirting corpse in bloody viscera.

No/yes, probably I would/would not.

89.

Oh, I Think He Will

Moving at a pace
With no particular thought
He strides along
A shadow to attract no interest.

Down the Embarcadero
To Aquatic Park
The Marina and Crissy Field
Out to windy Fort Point.

Beneath the bridge
He observes the massive single span
Crossing the Golden Gate
Deep dark ebb tide running swift.

He walks up the path
Amongst the dense foliage
Up to the pedestrian walkway
That leads out onto the bridge.

90.

On a roll

Way we go
On a ro'
See the goal
Feel no woe
Got this bo'
By the toe
Goes by Mo
Room to grow
Like a pro
Don't say no
So-and-so
Legs a bow
Long hot pole
Shovelling coal
Got some soul
Ass like dough
Up his hole
Like a mole
Or a vole
Takes its toll
Oh, so droll
Nice and slow
Pretty ho'
Ain't no foe
Bitch and co
Eat his roe

Eat no crow

Pissing po'

Ain't got no dough

Don't come

No Mo.

91.

Early Night

Wandering the streets like some zombie
I thought I can't go on like this
But I do somehow go on like this
And this is what it often is these days
Wandering about not quite alive.

Thinking of the lives of those dead ones
I make tea I don't really want
Look at the pen in my hand
And with nothing much left to say
Stare beyond the window.

I regret nothing I say
Though the voice says shit you regret everything
I smile but it is not so funny
Straightening the edge of the curtain
I think about an early night.

92.

Life Verses Happiness

When young he thought life was all about happiness
That life meant happiness
A life of happiness
The pursuit of happiness
Happy to do to think to feel.

Had he been wrong in his thinking?
Had he been naïve?
Older he no longer felt thought or did much happiness
While happiness affiliates gave little to no pleasure.

He examined carefully his full and empty life
Where he detected a great something obscuring happiness
With pain in mind pain in heart.

He thought he must return his life to basics
Find again that happiness he used to know.

Too late perhaps for he is accustomed to non-happiness.

93.

Disingenuous What

Mental illness can be a problem
But where possible
Keep the lid on.

With no reason
No reason to discuss
Mental conditions.

Art involvement
Generally speaking
The merchandise of mental illness.

No marginalization
Mad bad fag-art category
Take your 50% cut and go.

Artwork therapy
Keeping horrors at bay
Fighting existence.

No reason to portray
Any particular image
Why bother.

What happiness

What enjoyment
In only what needs to be done.

Some liked some detested
Destroyed or worked over
What interest seeing them again.

Sex inspiration
An act the orgasm
The sex-death-combo.

Long pig man
Needs any hole
To shove it.

Portraits of worth
No portrait worth money
Sold all the same.

Correct opening
Opening private thoughts
To public view.

Art detestation
Art instability
Art galleries cause illness.

Live cheaply
Income precarious

Nothing superfluous.

No electronic noise
No sounds
No stinking vehicle.

British art school in the 70's
Major Country Awards for the asking
Brats bankrolled through the system.

Teaching art
A slow
Painful suicide.

The painting hung
The picture slips
A loose noose.

Some debt
A favour returned
In cash for Dilly dick.

He will not tell
No one speaks
They all have fucking Kray stories.

Reputation
Good agent
Right place right time scenario.

Do not fuss
Just squirt it
From the tube.

Sick daddy genius gene
Fight it
Or it may finish you.

Kick your butt
Smothered in sleep
Squeezed out brain.

Art is not hard
Smash it up
Do it again.

Pick up a pen
Just wait
Shit will always out.

Voice
Does not change
It gets gruff.

"We have reason to believe
That you are in receipt
Of stolen property."

Them-there 500 brushes

Them-there 600 tubes of paint
Professionally sucked and fucked for.

Greed and power
Grief and pain
And that's about what all life is.

94.

I Have It All

I have the shrieking voices
Hell-like visions
I have the mind twisting neurosis
The soul blistering fits
I have the foul demented murder
The stench of rotting flesh
I have a senior pass to ride the bus.

95.

None but the Dead

None were old
None ready to die
Was it all a terrible mistake?
Some twisted joke?

"People die all the time"
You say,
"Every second
What's the big deal?"

But have you held the dying?
Those whom you kissed and fucked
Wiped their arses and their tears
Laughed and loved them unto death.

96.

Trouble Brewing

When the vague forms move in the kitchen
When the demon's sing aloud
When the shadow grabs your ankle in the shower
Then trouble again you know.

You sink fast praying into the unknown
To make the unbearable pass
You take the pills and swig the potion
Lie on the floor and wait.

Do not look at the man on the road to Damascus
Do not think of the wounds and death
Stay motionless and ignore the noises
Do not look at the clawing visions behind the eyes.

In the meantime you are a loony
You must shut your mind and mouth
Stop your eyes and brain
Sleep or suicide are your options.

97.

U Flesh My Gun

U come at me" *Ur!*
"U can't do nuffin
"*Urr!*"
U slam me like a child
"*Urrr!*"
U dunk me like a drunk
"*Urrrr!*"

U leave no mark on me
I would take out my gun
I blow U brains out
I blow U away
Back where U belong.

U must learn to kill
Bite the charm
With defence classes
As posted
For those about to die.

See the men
With long clubs and shields
By the maudlin wall
Watching for the stones to fall.

Face the bombs

Face the grace

Get through U life . . .

And don't say no little prayer for me.

98.

Oakland Bad Boys - 1979

"I ain't yo
Niggy-Wiggy."

"Then I'm not your
Honky-Wonky."

"Yo *is* my Honky-Wonk."

"Then you must be my Niggy-Wig."

"You're just my black-boy fuck-toy," I goad him,
"You fuck black but cum white and bleed red."
He kisses me and slides off his condom
Holding me down he whispers, "I ain't *your* black-boy."
Slowly he empties the condom across our lips tonguing his sweet cum
into me
"Eat that black cum," he slobbers, "*my* white cum-boy."

"The Messiah when he cum, *my* white ass-boy" he says later,
"He-be-born, a *black-ass*-boy!"

"I'm not *your* white ass-boy," I say,
"But you're almost *my* inter-rimmed black Messiah-boy."
He grabs me, "And I'll own your blasphemous white ass, *boy*."
We wrestle and holla and fall off the bed
There we laugh at race religion the political lunacy

No shit like that when bad black an' white boys roll naked.

"What of your religion, politics and ethnicity now?"
"Shit! Holy shit! Holy cum! Holy cow!"

99.

Wasted Day

Head so thick
Cannot think
Chatting noises
Begin to sink.

Strings of words
Knots of blood
Déjà vu land
Sunk in mud.

Pop some pills
Feel okay
Going nowhere
Not today.

100

XXII. My Policeman Friend – Loss

My policeman friend spoke sad and low,

"You're not normal . . . you're not right in the fucking head."

"Yes, I know; we are both well aware of that."

"You're just blowing me off for no good reason, and I haven't even
done anything."

"You haven't," I said, "but I just can't do this anymore."

"Can't do *what* anymore? I told you I love you; I want us to live together .
. . we could be happy together . . . and you did, you told me you loved me,
and now you're blowing me off, just like that."

"I need to, for myself, for my own sanity."

"What the fuck is the matter with you? . . . Fucking, grow up will you!"

I watched my policeman friend's tears, the man I did love.

Watched him stride away out of my life.

I wanted to call out to him.

Wanted my arms about him.

Tell him not to cry it was all right and that I did love him and would live
with him forever, and for a day.

He would have loved that . . . but I could not move.

Then he was gone.

D. L. Forbes resides in California

Front cover: Author self-portrait, oils on canvas, 1967
Copyright © D. L. Forbes

Back cover: Photograph of author by Sarah Menefee, 2021
Copyright © Sarah Menefee

FOURBEESBOOKS
Poetry series
London, Edinburgh & San Francisco